Gayle Vanzino

Sweet & Simple Sewing

The Five Mile Press

The Five Mile Press Pty Ltd
1 Centre Road, Scoresby
Victoria 3179 Australia
www.fivemile.com.au

Craft editor: Kathreen Ricketson
Photography: Greg Elms Photography
Illustrations: Guy Holt
Additional images courtesy of Shutterstock
A CIP record is available from the
National Library of Australia
First published 2012
Printed in China 5 4 3 2 1

Contents

Introduction

Sewing is fun – and it's not hard to do. With a few simple stitches and a little imagination, you will be on your way to creating your own personalised pieces. You will learn to make your own clothes, shoes, bags and many other things which no one else will have. All the projects in this book can be quickly and easily made – many from just one rectangle of fabric or recycled materials that you can find around your home. Most of these pieces can be made by hand and only a few require a sewing machine. There is something here for everyone – from the very newest sewer to the more experienced. Make these funky creations for yourself, or give them as special handmade gifts to family and friends. Craft stores and fabric shops are a paradise of beautiful materials in countless colours and patterns – head out, find your look and get creative!

You will learn simple dressmaking techniques, embroidery stitches, how to appliqué, how to jazz up your old clothes, and much more. Soon you will be making many more projects of your own creation – because once you get bitten by the sewing bug, you'll never want to stop!

So grab some funky fabrics, pick up your sewing needles, and start creating your own sweet and simple projects!

Sewing basics

This is where the fun begins! In this chapter, you'll find everything you need to know about the equipment and basic techniques for making the fab creations in this book.

Gather your supplies

Basic sewing kit

No matter what type of sewing you are going to do, you will need some basic tools. You might have a few of these already around your house, or you may be able to borrow some of them from a more experienced sewer. Or, you might want to start collecting a few new items for your very own sewing kit. Here is a list to help you get started:

Scissors for cutting fabric
These usually have bent handles with blades about 20cm long. Your fabric scissors are your 'good' scissors, and you will need to keep them sharp – so use them for fabric only.

Scissors for paper
Use these for cutting out your paper templates.

Small sewing scissors
These are straight scissors and will come in really handy for cutting off threads, especially when hand sewing.

Pinking shears
These scissors create a zigzag edge, and are great for finishing seam allowances or making decorative edges.

Tape measure

A vinyl tape is best as it won't stretch. Hang it around your neck when you are sewing – this saves it from being lost or accidentally cut while you are working.

Hand sewing needles

Make a collection that includes several different sizes and types. Some embroidery needles (often called crewels) are also good to have.

Sewing machine needles

If you are planning to sew with stretch fabrics, you will definitely need some ballpoint needles. Check the machine manual for the recommended brand of needles and keep a collection of ballpoint needles and regular needles in different sizes.

Pins

Glass headed pins are easy to see in your fabric. These are useful for temporarily holding your fabric together while you sew.

Pin cushion

The best place to keep your pins! You'll be making your very own pin cushion with the materials provided with this book.

Seam ripper

Mistakes happen to everyone! If you have to unpick whatever you've just sewn, a seam ripper is the safest way of getting the job done without damaging your fabric.

Thimble

A thimble is usually worn on the third finger of the hand that does the stitching, and provides protection for your finger as it pushes the needle through the fabric.

2B pencil

Great to make a mark on fabrics as it washes out easily. You could also use marking chalk.

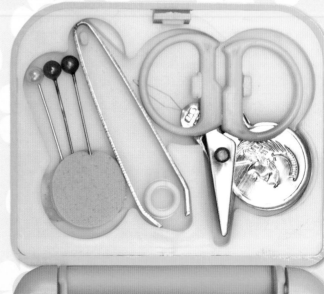

Mini kit

Mini kits are really handy as they contain everything you need for small sewing jobs, like fixing holes, hems or loose buttons.

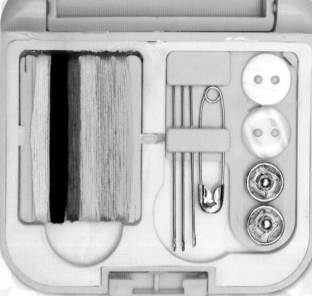

Other bits

Buttons, beads, appliqué patches, ribbons and funky threads – in sewing terms, these are known as **notions**. Start collecting interesting bits that you can use to decorate your sewing projects.

Threads

This topic could fill up its own chapter! But here are the basics:
• Match your thread to your fabric, so the fabric and thread will shrink at the same rate when you wash your item.
• When sewing cotton fabric, use cotton thread.
• When sewing poly/cotton or polyester fabric, use polyester thread.
• When sewing stretch fabric, use polyester thread.
• When colour matching, choose thread a slightly lighter shade than your fabric.
• Top stitch thread is slightly thicker and shows up more for embroidery.
• Embroidery thread is usually cotton and comes in skeins. You can separate the threads to use as few or as many as you like at once.
• Use good quality thread so your projects won't fall apart!

Where to keep your kit?

Here are just a few ideas:

• A plastic lunch box. Find an old one no longer in use, or pick up something bright and new from the supermarket.

• A cardboard shoebox. You can decorate it to make your very own personalised sewing box.

• A fishing tackle box (preferably one that hasn't been used for fishing!)

• A small suitcase

• A special sewing box. These can be purchased from any craft or fabric store.

Tip
Be on the lookout for useful bits for your sewing collection. Have your friends and family donate old clothes, or rummage through second hand shops for fabrics, trims, buttons, beads, lace and ribbons. Make sure you always wash second hand items before using them.

Choosing fabrics

Head into any fabric store, and the choice of materials can be overwhelming! But it doesn't have to be tricky to choose exactly what you need.

Tip
Choose fabrics with a pattern that runs both ways, so you don't have to worry about matching the patterns when joining pieces together.

Woven fabrics

Have you ever done paper weaving? You made a 'loom' by making some even slits into a square of paper, and then used coloured strips of paper to weave in and out across the loom to make a pattern. This is the basic technique that is used by machines to make woven fabrics. The paper strips still attached to the 'loom' is the **warp** thread and the separate strips woven in and out across the loom are the **weft** threads. All woven fabrics are made up of two yarns which are woven together on a machine loom. The warp threads are those which run parallel to the selvedge (see page 15). The weft threads run across the fabric from selvedge to selvedge. You'll get a closer look at these warp and weft threads when you make the Summer Scarf (see page 40). Some examples of woven fabrics include calico, drill, poplin, denim and quilting fabric.

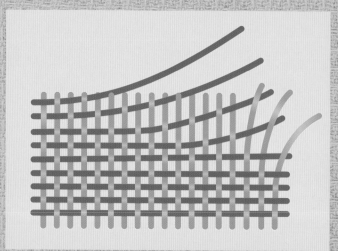

Knitted fabrics

Knitted fabrics are made from just one yarn that is knitted by machine in much the same way as woolly scarves and jumpers are made with knitting needles. Knitted fabrics are usually very stretchy and are great for making tops and sports wear. You'll see how easy stretch fabrics are to sew when you make the Tube Tops (see page 24 and 26). Some examples of knitted fabrics include spandex, jersey, lycra, velour and polar fleece.

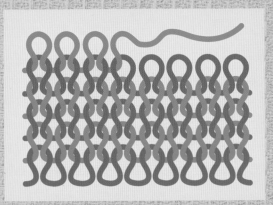

Tip
Most of the projects in this book are made from either woven or knitted fabrics. Each project will have instructions on the best fabric to use.

Using a sewing machine

There are many different types of sewing machines – from simple straight sewers to complicated computerised models! If you haven't used a machine before, here are some ideas to help you along:
• ask an experienced sewer for lessons
• read the manual that came with your sewing machine
• look online for information
• check your local library for instructional books

Here are a few useful sewing machine tips:
• lower the presser foot onto your fabric first, then lower the needle into your work
• always hold upper and lower threads at back of your work as you start sewing
• guide fabrics gently without pulling
• for straight stitching, adjust stitch length before you sew
• for zigzag stitching, adjust both stitch width and length before you sew
• always place pins perpendicular to the direction of your stitching, so that your machine needle can sew over them (at slow speed). You don't want to break your needle by trying to sew over a pin head!

Getting started
Your sewing space

Okay – you have your sewing kit, you've collected some cool fabrics, and you're ready to go. All that you need now is space to sew!

If you are hand sewing:
• find a comfortable chair
• check you have good lighting
• keep a rubbish bin nearby
• keep your sewing kit close so that everything you need will be within arms reach

Tip
If your project calls for the use of an iron, check with an adult in your house before using it.

If using a sewing machine:
• ask an adult to help you set it up at a table or desk that has a comfortable chair and good lighting
• check the machine is working properly by sewing on a scrap of fabric with straight stitch (check for even tension and a medium stitch length). Then sew with a zigzag stitch (check for even tension and wide stitch width)
• insert a new machine needle and keep a few spares handy

Basic sewing terms

There may be some words in this book you have never heard of before. Here are a few explanations to help you out.

Selvedge:
This is the finished edge of the fabric along each side of the length (straight grain) of the fabric. The selvedges run parallel to the warp threads. These selvedges should always be cut off for making most projects – especially clothes.

Grain: The warp threads run parallel to the selvedge. This is the straight grain of your fabric (see page 12).

Ease: the extra centimetres added to clothing patterns to allow wearing comfort as your body moves. More ease is required for woven fabrics than knitted fabrics because knitted fabrics already have some stretch built in to them. Without ease, clothes would be very tight and uncomfortable.

Seam: This is a line of stitching which joins two fabrics together.

Seam allowance: The space between the line of stitching joining two fabrics together and the raw (or cut) edge.

Right side of fabric:
The side of fabric on which the pattern is printed. It is usually more brightly coloured than the wrong side.

Wrong side of fabric:
The underside of fabric. The pattern is not as brightly coloured on this side, or there may be no pattern at all.

Press cloth:
This is a cloth that has been impregnated with special chemicals. It is placed over the item you wish to iron to protect the fabric from scorching. If you do not have a press cloth, you can use a large handkerchief or other large cotton square.

Threading a needle

Hold the end of the thread between your lips. Measure out enough thread to fit approximately from your middle finger to your elbow, and cut this length. Flatten out the end of the thread with your lips and gently push it through the eye of the needle. Tie a knot in the end of your thread, and you are ready to sew!

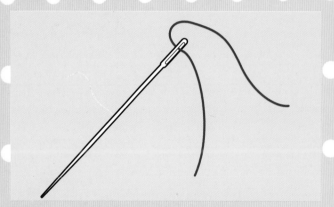

Tip
If you make the thread too long it can be difficult to sew. Also, the longer the thread, the more easily it can knot or tangle.

Basic stitches
Sewing a running stitch

A running stitch makes a line of 'dashes', and can be used to hold fabrics together as well as for decoration. Push the needle from the back of the fabric, up through the front of the fabric. Push the needle back down through the fabric and then up again to make a stitch.

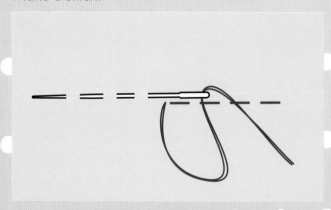

Sewing a backstitch

This stitch makes a long unbroken line of stitching, and is used to make a strong seam. Push the needle from the back of the fabric to the front. Take the needle back a couple of millimetres, depending on how big you want your stitch, and then push needle back through the fabric and then up again a couple of millimeters in front of your last stitch.

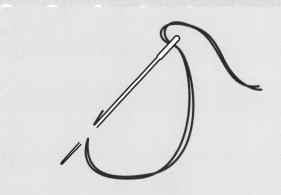

Sewing a blanket stitch

This stitch is used to make decorative edges as well as to hold fabrics together. Push the needle from the back to the front of the fabric. Push the needle down through the fabric a couple of millimetres to the right. Bring needle back up just below it but make sure you have the caught the loose thread. Push the needle down through the fabric a couple of millimetres to the right.

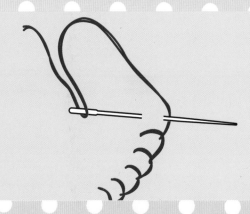

Sewing a chain stitch

This is a great stitch for decorative embroidery. Push the needle from the back to the front of the fabric. Now push the needle down through the fabric, just beside the place where the needle came up. Then come up just below this spot, and make sure you hold the thread to make a loop.

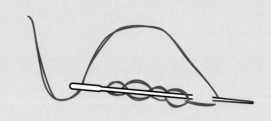

Sewing a feather stitch

This is a great stitch for decoration – especially appliqué. It is done in two stages but is very easy. Push the needle up through the fabric, and then take your thread down to the right (A). Come up over the thread and pull through (B). Now go to the left, down into the fabric (C), and up again over the thread (D). Pull the thread through. Repeat both stitches.

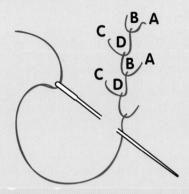

How to measure your body

It is always easier to have another person take your measurements. Have your measuring tape, a notepad and pencil handy. Wear your normal undergarments, stand up tall, and look straight ahead. Here are a few measurements you need to have for projects in this book:

Underarm: Right around your body at the armpit level
Chest: Right around your body at the point of bust level
Waist: Right around your body around your belly button.
High hip: Right around your body at the hip bone level
Low hip: Right around your body almost over the buttocks
Length: Usually, you will need to try the garment on to make this decision

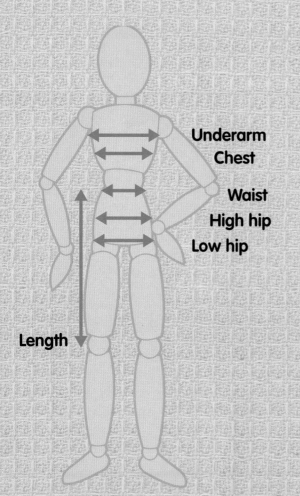

Underarm
Chest

Waist
High hip
Low hip

Length

Once you have decided on the project you wish to create – make sure you read all the instructions first. Next, assemble all the items and fabrics you will need. Take a deep breath, and follow the steps one by one. Take your time with all the projects – and remember, everyone makes mistakes! The more you practice, the quicker you will sew and the more amazing your creations will be.

Congratulations – you are ready to start sewing!

Sewing on buttons

A few of the projects in this book will require you to sew on buttons – to fasten an opening, or simply to add cool decorations! Learning to sew buttons is really handy – so here's how:

1. Thread a sewing needle with cotton and tie a knot in the end. Make sure your sewing needle is small enough to fit through the holes in your buttons.

2. Push the needle through your fabric from the back to the front in the spot where you want to place your button.

3. Push the needle through one button hole. Then, pass the needle to the back of your fabric through the second button hole.

4. Repeat a few times, up through one button hole and down through the other, until your button feels tight and secure.

5. When you are happy that your button is secure, push the needle through to the back of your fabric and sew a few stitches to hold your thread. Cut the thread with your small scissors.

The Projects

Now that you have learned the basics, it's time to put your cool new skills into action!

Drawstring top

This top is easy to make, fun to wear, and you only need a small amount of fabric. You could even recycle an old shirt or dress!

What you'll need

- Approx 60–70 cm of fabric, 100–110 cm wide
- Sewing machine or sewing needles
- Thread to match your fabric
- Fabric scissors
- Ruler and pencil
- Sewing pins and a large safety pin
- Ribbon for drawstrings

Measurements

Follow the instructions on how to measure on page 19

Width: Chest measurement + 8 cm for ease + 4 cm for seam allowances = fabric width

Length: Measure from underarms to waist + 5 cm for ease + 8 cm for casings top and bottom = fabric length

1. Lay your fabric out and use your measuring tape to mark your width and length. Use pins to mark these. Use a ruler and pencil to draw a line between the pin markings. Cut the rectangle of fabric.

2. Fold your fabric right sides together, short edges lined up. Pin in place. Measure 8 cm from both the upper and the lower edges and mark with a pencil.

3. Using a straight stitch on your sewing machine, and a 2 cm seam allowance (see page 15), sew the fabric together. Begin at the 8 cm marked point and end at the marked point at the other end. Give a small reverse stitch to strengthen the seam endings. Trim each raw seam edge with pinking shears to prevent fraying.

FOLD

8 cm

SEW

8 cm

5. Pin the fabric on the pressed un-sewn 8 cm gap at the top and bottom. Then using the straight stitch, stitch in 1 cm from the open edge, down towards the side seam, across the seam, then up again towards the raw edge. Repeat with the other pressed open seam.

4. Use a hot iron to press open the seam. Make sure you also press the un-sewn section open.

Tip
Be very careful when using the hot iron. Ask for help if you need it.

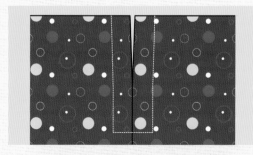

6. To make your casings for the drawstring, fold one raw edge over 4 cm and pin in place. Stitch 1/2 cm away from the raw edge, and then 1/2 cm away from the folded edge. Repeat this with the other raw edge. Press flat with an iron.

7. Take one of the ribbons and attach a large safety pin to one end. Thread the pin through one casing, and use the pin to help you move the fabric along the ribbon. Repeat this with the other ribbon and casing.

Draw up the ends and try the top on. Tighten the strings to fit yourself, tie them up, and away you go!

Tube top

This great top uses just one rectangle of fabric. You should be able to make two tops from the one length of fabric as knit fabric is usually 150 cm wide. Two for the price of one – hooray!

What you'll need

- Approx 50 cm of two-way stretch knit fabric
- Thread to match your fabric
- 3.5 cm wide non-roll elastic to fit around your chest and waist + 1 cm for join
- Sewing machine
- Fabric scissors
- Felt tip pen
- Ballpoint sewing machine
- Needles
- Sewing pins

Measurements

Follow the instructions on how to measure on page 19

Width: Chest measurement + 2 cm seam allowance = fabric width

Length: Measure from underarms to waist + 10 cm for casings = fabric length

1. Lay out your fabric so that the greatest amount of stretch will go around your body (this is your width). Measure and cut your width and length of fabric.

2. Fold your fabric along the width, right sides together, and pin. Raise the presser foot on your sewing machine, place fabric under using a 1 cm seam allowance, and lower the foot. Set your machine to a medium zigzag stitch and lower the needle into the fabric. As you sew, make sure to slightly stretch the fabric. You will now have a tube shape.

3. Measure the elastic around your chest. Pull it so it has a comfortable stretch and then add 1 cm. Cut the elastic and then repeat with your waist. Use a black felt tip pen to mark each one: chest and waist. Pin each piece of elastic end to end to create two circles. Stitch each circle together using the zigzag stitch.

4. Measure 5 cm down from both the upper and lower edges of your fabric tube. Use a pencil to mark the 5 cm mark.

5. Fold over the marked 5 cm of fabric to create a casing for the elastic. As you are folding, place the elastic inside the casing and pin the fabric down, making sure you don't catch

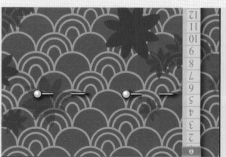

the elastic in the pins. The elastic will be smaller than the fabric, so you will need to stretch the elastic to fit around the top.

6. Place the raw seam of the casing under the presser foot select a zigzag stitch with a medium width and small length. Lower the needle into the fabric and begin with a few small stitches. Stretch the fabric and elastic as you sew, holding the fabric from behind the needle with one hand and in front of the needle with the other hand. Zigzag right around the upper and lower edge of your top, fully encasing the elastic as you go, but be careful not to catch the elastic in the stitching!

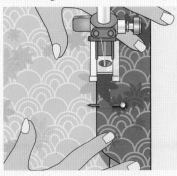

Turn your top inside out and – congratulations! You're done!

Tube top with ribbing

The use of stretch cotton makes this top easy to wear and simple to whip up. Choose a stretch fabric with a one-way stretch. This project is perfect for recycling an old T-shirt – you'll just need to buy some new ribbing.

What you'll need

- Approx 40 cm of cotton one-way stretch fabric
- 30 cm of cotton ribbing
- Sewing machine
- Threads to match your fabric
- Fabric scissors
- Ballpoint sewing machine needles
- Sewing pins

Measurements

Follow the instructions on how to measure on page 19

Width: Chest measurement + 4 cm for ease + 2 cm seam allowance = fabric width

Length: Measure from underarms to waist + 1 cm seam allowance, then minus 14 cm (this will be made up by 7 cm of ribbing top and bottom)

1. Lay out your fabric and pull it to find which direction has the greatest amount of stretch. This will go around your body (the width). Mark your measured width with a pin or a pencil. Then measure your length and mark. Cut out this rectangle of fabric.

2. The length of the ribbing needs to be approximately two thirds the size of the main fabric width. Work this out by taking your width measurement and dividing it by 3 then multiplying by 2. Ask for advice if you are unsure. Measure the ribbing along the stretchy length using your calculations above. Pin the ribbing together at the point of your measurement, but before cutting it, check that it will fit over your head and shoulders. Add extra length if it is too tight, or shorten it if it is too loose.

When you are happy with the fit, cut the ribbing at that point.

3. Next, you will need to divide the ribbing into 2 x 15 cm wide strips.

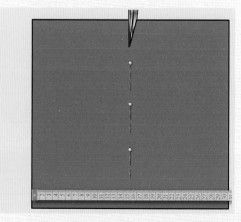

Tip
With all stretch fabrics make sure that the stretchy part goes around your body. You might need to experiment – tug your fabric a few times in different directions to see which way has the most stretch.

4. Take one strip of ribbing and fold it right sides together along the 15 cm edge. Pin in place. Using your sewing machine, sew a straight stitch with a 1/2 cm seam allowance. Press the seams open.
Turn the ribbing in so that the wrong sides are together. The seams should be inside facing each other.

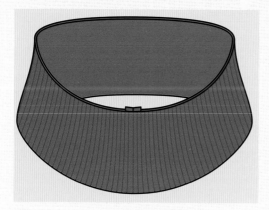

5. Pin the ribbing together at the seams. Then, lay it flat on the table with a pin at one side and another pin on the other side – now you have pins on the halfway points. Rotate the ribbing so that the pins are facing each other, and place another pin at each side to divide the circle of ribbing into quarters. Divide the other section of ribbing and the main section of fabric into quarters in the same way.

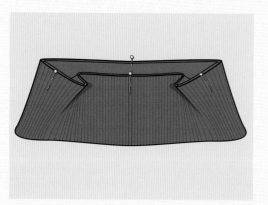

6. Line up the raw edges of the ribbing with one edge of the main section of fabric; make sure the right sides are facing each other. Match the seam pins, halfway point pins, and quarter mark pins. Repeat for the other end.

7. Add another set of pins in between the quarter mark pins, so you will have 8 pins around the circle. The ribbing may seem impossibly small for the top but when you stitch, the ribbing will stretch to fit.

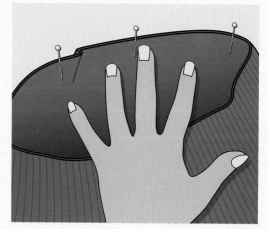

8. Place the pinned seams under the presser foot of your machine and lower the presser foot. Set the machine to a medium size zigzag stitch. Lower the needle into the fabric and do a few small stitches to begin, using a 1/2 cm seam allowance. Really stretch out both the ribbing and the main fabric as you zigzag them together. Stitch both the upper and lower edges of your top.

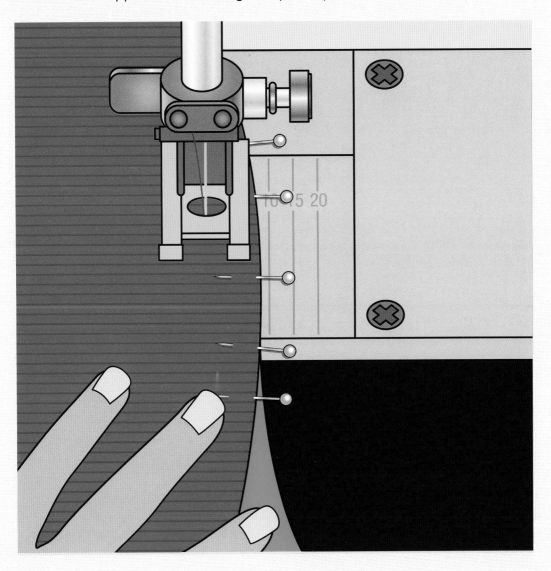

Turn your top right side out and wear it with pride! This top would be great over swimmers at the beach, or over a coordinated singlet top.

Mini skirt

A skirt is a great basic for any girl's wardrobe. Choose medium weight fabrics such as cotton, poly/cotton or lightweight denim.

What you'll need

- Approx 50 cm of 120 cm wide cotton fabric
- Thread to match
- Sewing machine
- Sewing pins
- Fabric scissors and pinking shears
- 3 cm wide elastic (length: around your waist + 1 cm)

Measurements

Follow the instructions on how to measure on page 19

Width: Measure around your widest part below the waist – this might be your high hip or low hip + 8 cm for ease + 2 cm seam allowance = fabric width

Length: Measure from your waist to the desired length (somewhere above your knees) + 5 cm for the elastic casing + 7 cm for the hem = fabric length

1. Lay out your fabric and measure your width and your length. Mark with a pencil. Cut out your rectangle.

2. Fold your fabric over, right sides together, so that the short sides line up. Pin together. Then machine sew using a straight stitch and a 1 cm seam allowance. Trim the raw edges of the seam with pinking shears to prevent fraying.

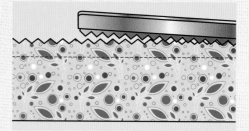

Press the seam open with a hot iron.

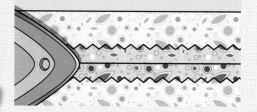

3. Use the pinking shears to trim 3 mm from both the top and bottom edges of your fabric.

4. To measure the elastic, hold it around your waist (slightly stretched) and add 1 cm for join. Cut at this point. Join the ends of the elastic together with a zigzag stitch on the sewing machine to create a circle. Make sure not to twist the elastic!

5. At the top of the skirt, create your casing for the elastic. Turn over 1 cm

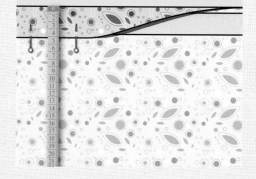

and press with a hot iron. Hold your circle of elastic against the top of the skirt, and fold the fabric again, this time over the elastic. Add 1/2 cm extra to give the elastic room to move and give you space to pin and sew. Pin the folded fabric down, making sure not to pin the elastic.

6. Now, sew the folded fabric down to enclose the elastic, but don't sew over the elastic. You may need to stretch the elastic as you go.

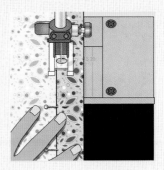

7. At the bottom of the skirt, measure 7 cm for the hem, fold it and pin. Machine stitch the hem 1/2 cm away from the pinked edge.

You're done! You can wear your gorgeous new skirt with your coordinated handmade tube top.

Sparkling singlet

You can personalise just about anything with a needle, thread and a little imagination! Here is one idea you can use to revamp an old T-shirt or singlet. Use beads from old jewellery, or purchase some new beads especially for the job.

What you'll need

- A singlet top or T-shirt
- Beads in various colours and sizes
- Hand sewing needle and strong thread

1. Thread a sewing needle and begin stitching at the top of the singlet neck with three firm backstitches. Take your first bead, and thread the needle through the bead from the neck edge of the singlet to where the neckband is stitched on.

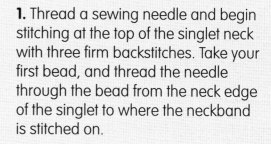

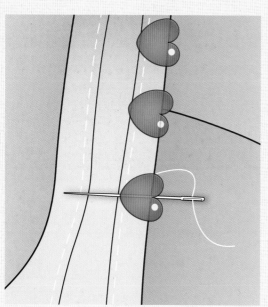

2. Push the needle through the band and back up to the neck edge and then thread on another bead.

3. When you get to the centre point of the singlet, try varying your pattern a little for some extra 'bling'.

4. Continue until you reach the other end of the singlet neck.

Tip
You can use beading to decorate any part of your singlet. Experiment with beads of different colours, sizes and shapes.

Beach dress

Want something easy to wear and quick to make? This cool dress is it! Choose any soft woven fabric with a nice bright print.

What you'll need

- Approx 80 x 120 cm piece of fabric (enough fabric to go around the widest part of your body one and half times + 4 cm seam allowance)
- 2 m of cotton cord
- Sewing machine
- Needles
- Matching thread
- Sewing pins
- Tape measure
- Fabric scissors

Measurements

Follow the instructions on how to measure on page 19

Width: The widest part of your body + half this again + 4 cm seam allowance = fabric width

Length: From underarms to your knees + 4 cm for casings + 2 cm for hem = fabric length

1. Lay out your fabric, with the grain running along your tabletop. Measure, mark and cut your length here.

2. Fold fabric in half along the length, with the right sides facing. Cut along the fold so that you now have two rectangles. Pin these two pieces together, right sides facing.

3. Measure and mark 14 cm up from the lower edge, and 16 cm down from the upper edge.

Tip
Choose a fabric with a simple pattern, or one that runs both ways across the fabric. This way you won't have any problems matching the front and back of your dress up when you sew the pieces together.

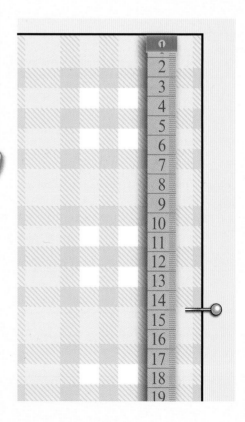

4. Stitch along both side seams between the marked points at the upper and lower edges, using a 1 cm seam allowance. Open out the seams and finish the raw edges with a zigzag stitch.

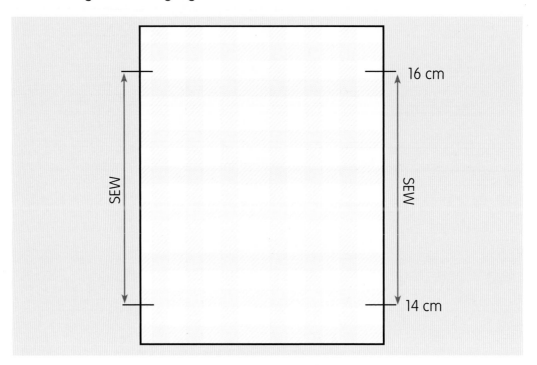

16 cm

SEW

SEW

14 cm

5. Press this seam open with an iron; continue pressing 1 cm under when you come to the open sections at the upper and lower edges of the dress. Using a straight stitch, stitch in 1 cm from the open edge, down towards the side seam, across the seam, then up again towards the raw edge. Repeat with the other pressed open seam.

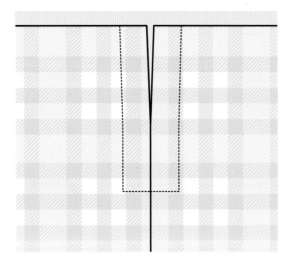

Tip
Zigzag stitching the top and bottom raw edges of the dress will prevent fraying.

6. Make the casings for the drawstrings at the upper edges by pressing under a 4 cm hem. Sew 1/2 cm from the folded edge and then at 1/2 cm from the zigzag edge.

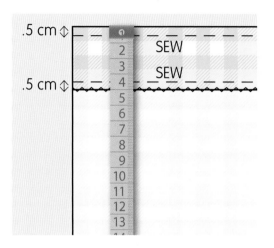

7. Put a safety pin through one end of your cotton cord and thread it through the front casing. Pull through until you have approximately 30 cm of cord left over at the end (this will make your shoulder straps). Repeat with back casing.

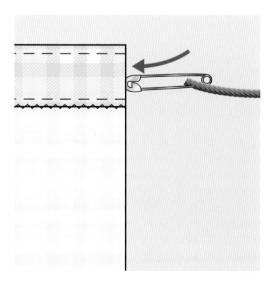

8. At the bottom hem edge, turn the fabric up 2 cm. Pin and use a straight stitch close to the zigzag stitching. Press.

Try on your dress on and tie up the straps. Grab your sunscreen and bathers and head to the beach!

Sarong

This is one of the easiest projects in the book – it can be made by hand or with a sewing machine. Choose any brightly-coloured fabric that has the print showing on both sides.

What you'll need

- Approx 1.6 m of 120 cm wide fabric such as cotton, poly/cotton or rayon (you will need enough to go around your body twice)
- Matching thread
- Sewing machine (optional)
- Needles
- Fabric scissors
- Sewing pins

3. Choose a way to wear your sarong!

Cute dress: Hold the sarong in front of you; the top centre should be above your chest. Wrap the two ends around the back of your body and bring to the front. Twist the ends and tie at your waist.

1. Lay out your fabric. Turn the raw edges of the fabric 1 cm under to the wrong side. Turn under again so that the edges are double folded. Pin into place.

2. If using a sewing machine: stitch along the folded hems 1 cm from the edge. If stitching by hand: use a running stitch 1 cm in from the edge of the hems.

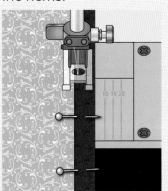

Cute top: Fold the sarong into a triangle shape, and then fold over the longest edge of the triangle a couple of times. Hold the centre of the triangle in front of your body then wrap the ends around your back. Bring the ends to your front, twist them and tie together at your waist.

Halter dress: Hold the centre of the sarong at the back of your body, bring the ends to the front and overlap them. Then twist the ends, take one end over one shoulder, and the other end over the other shoulder. Tie the ends behind your neck.

One-shoulder dress: Hold the centre of the sarong towards one side of your back. Wrap the ends around your body and bring one side across your front. Twist this end and place it under your arm, up over your shoulder and to the front again. Pull the other end around your body, twist the end and tie together.

Summer scarf

Summer scarves are great for adding colour to any outfit. Choose soft cottons, and be sure to check that your fabric has a pattern that shows on both sides.

What you'll need

- 30 cm of fabric at least 112 cm wide
- Fabric scissors
- A sewing pin
- Thread
- Sewing machine (optional) or sewing needles
- Tape measure
- 2B pencil and ruler

1. Spread your fabric out with the selvedge closest to you. Make a 5 cm snip through the selvedge about 1 cm in from the cut edge of the fabric. Tear the fabric from the snip right across the full width to the other selvedge. Repeat with the other cut edge.

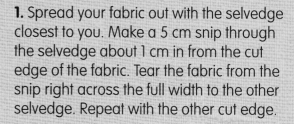

2. Cut 1 cm off from each of the selvedges.

3. Measure 2 cm in from the edge all the way around your scarf. Use your pencil to mark this line at intervals. Then use a ruler to lightly draw a line between your marks. This will be your sewing line.

Using your sewing machine and a straight stitch (or stitch by hand using running stitch), sew right around your scarf along your sewing line.

4. Grab a sewing pin and a comfy chair – fraying the edges will take a little time. Using your pin, gently tease out a few threads along one torn edge and pull the threads away from the scarf. Only pull out two or three threads each time. Continue pulling

out threads until the depth of the fringing is about 1 cm.

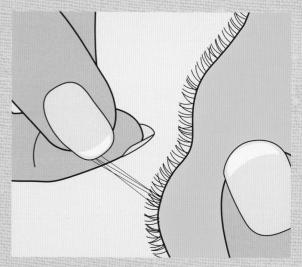

Repeat along the four edges of your scarf so that each edge has a fringe.

Give your scarf a quick press with a hot iron. Wear it tied around your neck, or use it as a headband with your favourite outfit!

Tip
Remember we talked about warp and weft threads in the introduction? You should be able to see these clearly in your frayed edges.

Scuffs

These scuffs are really simple to make – the hardest part is keeping your balance while tracing around your foot! Decorate them with buttons, felt or appliqué patches.

What you'll need

- An old towel (approx 20 x 20 cm)
- A piece of thick plastic (the insert from a reusable shopping bag works well)
- A square of craft felt (30 x 30 cm)
- A piece of cardboard big enough for you to stand on
- A small piece of wadding, extra towelling or an old blanket
- Fabric scraps for appliqué (optional)
- Matching thread
- Sewing pins
- Sewing needles
- Fabric and paper scissors
- Pencil
- Tape measure

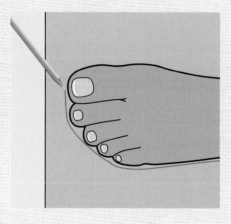

1. Place your foot on the cardboard and ask a friend to trace around both of your feet. Draw a curve over the top of all your toes. Measure and draw an extra 1 cm out from your foot outline, and cut out around the larger tracing – you now have your pattern.

2. Use the pattern to cut out your two feet from the towel and from the felt. Make sure you have a left and a right!

3. Next, take one cardboard foot pattern, and cut off the 1 cm allowance. Use this pattern to cut out the plastic and the wadding – flip the pattern to make sure you have a left and right foot.

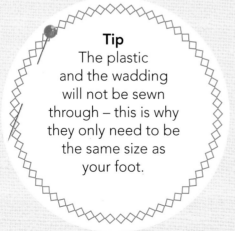

Tip
The plastic and the wadding will not be sewn through – this is why they only need to be the same size as your foot.

4. While you are standing, measure across the widest part of your foot from the floor over your foot and to the floor again. Add 2 cm for seam allowance. This will be your band length. From towelling, cut two bands 10 cm wide x the length you have measured above.

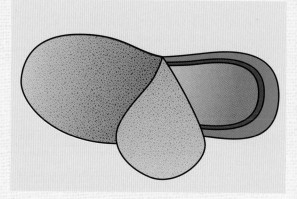

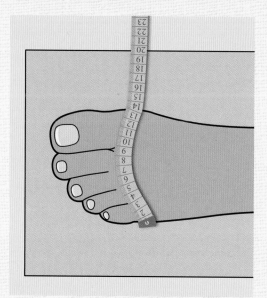

8. Carefully place your foot on one 'scuff sandwich' (without disturbing the layers) and decide where you want the band to go. Pin it into place. Use pins to secure the toweling and felt layers around the whole scuff. Repeat on your other foot.

5. If you are doing the appliqué, now is the time to attach you motifs: fold the bands in half to find the centre, pin the motifs on, then hand stitch in place.

6. Turn over a 1 cm hem along both lengths of the bands, and pin into place. You can sew this by hand using a running stitch, or a straight stitch on your sewing machine.

7. Put your layers together: start with the felt, then the plastic, then the wadding, and finish with the towelling.

9. Make a double strand of thread in a colour that matches the towelling. Begin with a knot and three firm backstitches, then push the needle through from the felt back to the towelling front. Remember, you are not sewing through the middle two layers, only the outer layers. Return by pushing the needle through from the towelling to the felt. Continue until you have sewn around the entire scuff. If sewing by machine, insert a zipper foot. Stitch in 1 cm from the outer edge all the way around the scuff, removing any pins as you go.

10. If sewing by hand, you will need two rounds of stitches. This time, push the needle through from the towelling side to the felt in an existing hole and back through again to make the stitching look like machine backstitching.

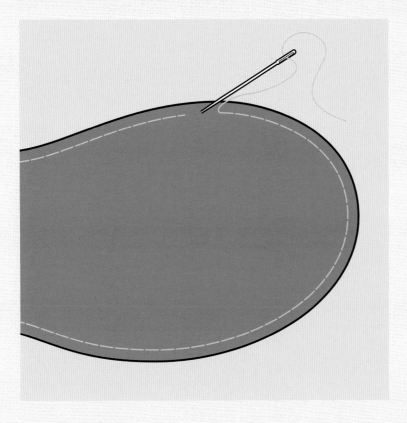

11. Once you have stitched all the way around, trim off any loose threads – and start dancing!

Tip
Take a little extra time when you reach the bands, as there are more layers to sew through.

Beach bag

This handy bag can be whipped up in no time at all – and if you're in a rush to get to the beach, all you need is a towel!

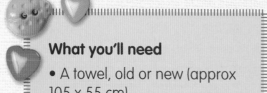

What you'll need

• A towel, old or new (approx 105 x 55 cm)

• Approx 112 cm of medium weight rope (enough to fit across the towel twice with some overhang)

• Measuring tape

• Sewing needle or sewing machine

• Thread

• Sewing pins

3. Measure the rope before cutting it – check that it fits across the top edge of the towel twice with a 12 cm overhang.

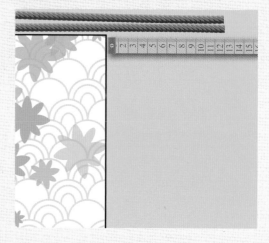

1. Fold the towel in half matching the short ends together (right sides facing if your towel has a pattern on one side). Measure 10 cm down from the top (where the open edges meet). Mark with a pin at both sides of the towel.

2. Stitch along both sides of the towel using a backstitch, starting from your marked 10 cm point to the fold of the towel. Turn right side out.

4. Fold the top edge of the towel down 5 cm to create a casing for the rope. Place the rope inside this fold. Pin the rope inside, then stitch down the top of the towel on both the front and back of the bag, but don't stitch the rope – it needs to move smoothly inside the casing.

Tie the end of the rope together and pack your things!

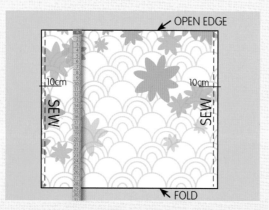

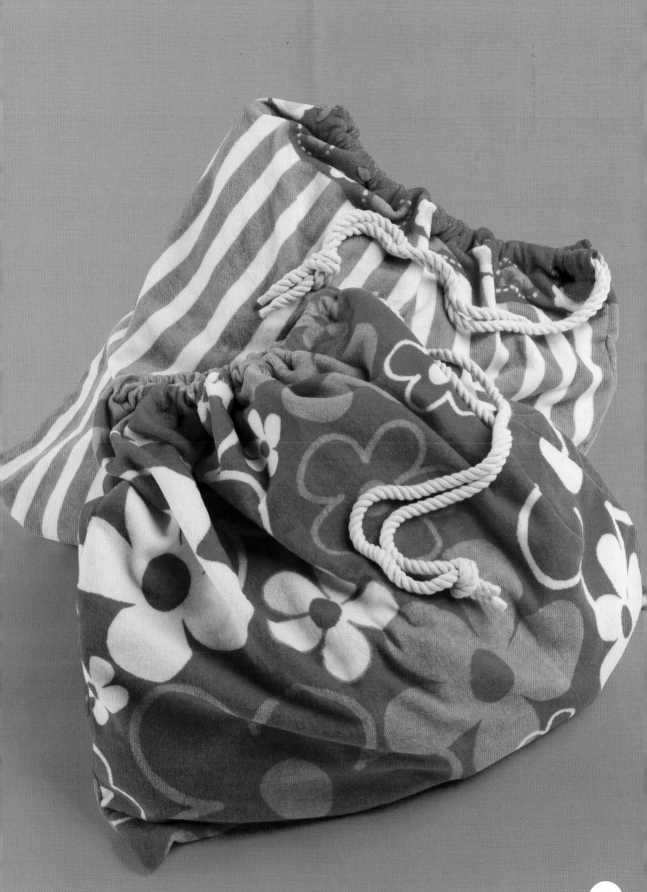

Tote bag

With a little imagination and a few stitches, you can recycle lots of items in your wardrobe. This cute bag is made from an old pair of jeans! You can decorate it with buttons, beads or ribbon – be as creative as you like.

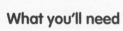

What you'll need

- An old pair of jeans
- Approx 50 cm of cotton fabric for lining
- Sewing machine
- Sewing pins
- Fabric scissors
- Thread
- Ruler and 2B Pencil
- Decorative buttons

1. Using your ruler and pencil, mark a line across the top of each of the jean legs (approx 3 cm down from the crotch seam).

Pin, and then use your sewing machine to sew through both sides of the jeans leg along this line.

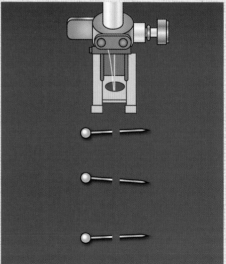

2. Mark another line 10 cm down from your stitching. Cut off both legs at this point. Fold the jeans legs up twice (each fold 5 cm) to make cuffs. Press into place with a hot iron.

3. Measure your jeans to make sure the lining will fit:

Width
Measure the widest part of jeans (this is probably the leg section) + add 2 cm seam allowance = fabric width

Length
Measure from the top of the waist band to the stitched line + 3 cm = fabric length

4. From your lining fabric cut out two rectangles using these measurements.

5. Place your lining pieces right sides together, line up the edges and pin along the short sides. Using a straight stitch on your sewing machine (and a 1 cm seam allowance), sew down one short side, along one long side and up the other short side to make the bag lining.

6. Take the open edge at the top and turn it under 2 cm all around, wrong side to wrong side. Pin it all around, but do not turn it right side out.

7. Make your loop: Cut a piece of spare lining fabric 10 x 5 cm, then use an iron to fold the long edges into the centre, wrong side to wrong side. Fold this in half again and machine stitch together. Or, simply use a piece of cord or ribbon.

8. Place your lining inside the bag. The wrong sides of the lining should be touching the wrong side of the bag. Match up the side seams of the lining and the bag.

9. You will need to make a few tucks at the top to make your lining fit the 'waist' of your jeans. Pin the lining in place at quarter intervals. Then, every 10 cm or so, make a little pleat and pin in place. Do this all around until the lining is evenly arranged. When you are happy with the fit, pin the loop at the centre back between the lining and the jeans.

10. Hand sew around the top of the lining to attach it to the bag. You don't need to stitch all the way through the denim – just enough to secure the lining to the bag.

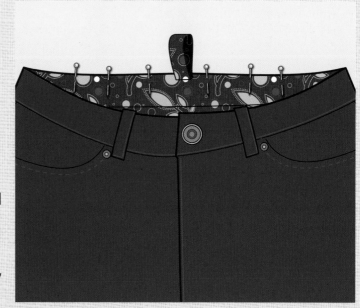

11. Using the leftover jeans legs, measure and cut 5 cm wide strips for the handle. You'll want the handle to be about 100 cm long, so you may need to join two or more strips together.

12. Cut a piece of lining fabric the same size as your handle. Pin the two strips of fabric together wrong side to wrong side, then sew using a straight stitch on your sewing machine. Pull out a few threads from the edges to slightly fray the seams for decoration.

Tip
Check the length of the handle you want by measuring over your shoulder to your hips.

13. Pin the handle to the outside of the side seams of your bag and machine sew in place.

Pack with your favourite things, and be sure to tell your friends that you recycled!

Reversible shoulder bag

Coordinating your accessories and clothes is no problem with this reversible bag! You can be extra creative and do some patchwork or appliqué on the pockets, or you can keep it as simple as you like.

What you'll need

- 50 cm of 112–120 cm wide cotton fabric (main fabric)
- 50 cm of 112–120 cm wide cotton fabric (second contrast fabric)
- 2 toggle buttons (or buttons of your choice)
- 10 cm each of four different fabrics for patchwork and appliqué (optional)
- 20 x 30 cm lightweight wadding (if doing patchwork)
- Small piece of double sided fusible interfacing (if doing appliqué)
- Sewing machine
- Sewing thread
- Sewing pins
- 2B Pencil
- Ruler
- Fabric scissors & paper scissors

Patchwork:

A. From each of the patchwork fabrics cut one strip 5.5 x 30 cm.

B. Follow the process for strip piecing as per the patchwork cushion cover (see page 62), cutting strips to 7.5 cm long after stitching them together

C. Pin your wadding to the back of the patchwork. Then use a ruler and pencil to mark diagonal lines across the patchwork, ensuring that the ruler lines up with the corners on each patch. Use a straight stitch on your sewing machine to stitch along the ruled lines, through both the wadding and the patchwork piece.

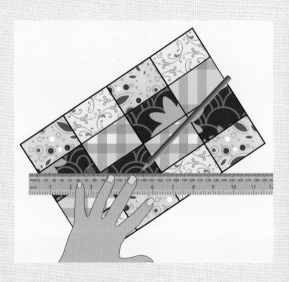

1. From both the main fabric and the contrast fabric, cut each of the following:
One rectangle 36 x 80 cm (bag piece)
One strip the full width of fabric 112–120 cm long x 7 cm wide (handle)
One rectangle 20 x 30 cm (pocket)
One rectangle 12 x 5 cm (loop)

Tip:
Appliqué or patchwork pockets are optional – omit these steps if you are not doing the appliqué or patchwork.

D. Place your patchwork piece on top of your cutout plain pocket piece of fabric, 1/2 cm in from the edge, and with right sides facing. Pin together. Stitch along three sides leaving the bottom edge open to turn right side out.

E. Trim the corners by snipping diagonally across the seam allowance (but not through the stitching), then turn the pocket right side out.

F. Use a hot iron to press the unstitched side 1/2 cm in on both the patchwork and the pocket edges. Pin into place and stitch together close to the folded edges, removing the pins as you go.

G. Position your now quilted pocket onto your bag fabric and pin around three sides. Stitch into place.

Appliqué:

A. Take your double sided fusible interfacing and find the shiny side. Draw any shapes you like onto the smooth side of the interfacing, then use paper scissors to cut out the shapes.

B. Lay the interfacing shapes, rough side down, onto the wrong side of your fabric scraps. Use an iron to fuse the sticky side of the paper onto your fabric. Leave it for a minute to cool down.

C. Take your sewing scissors and carefully cut out your fabric shapes. Remove the paper backing, and you will see a shiny residue on the back of the fabric. Place this side down onto your pocket piece.

D. Use your iron to gently press your shapes for a minute or two until they stick properly.

E. Now, grab your coloured threads and your sewing needle – choose any stitches you like to frame the appliqué patches on your pocket.

F. After completing your appliqué, hem around the pocket piece by making a double fold around all four edges, and press. Stitch across the top hem of the pocket only, then position the pocket onto your bag piece and place pins around three sides of the pocket. Sew into place with a straight stitch on your sewing machine.

To make plain pockets:

A. Take your pocket pieces and make a double fold around all four edges. Press into place with a hot iron.

B. Stitch across the folds using a straight or zigzag stitch on your sewing machine (or a hand sewn running stitch).

C: Position the pocket onto the bag fabric piece and pin into place, then use a straight stitch on your sewing machine to sew the three sides into place, leaving the top side open.

4. Place the two long strips of fabric for the handle together, right sides facing. Using a straight stitch on your sewing machine, sew along each side, leaving the ends open for turning.

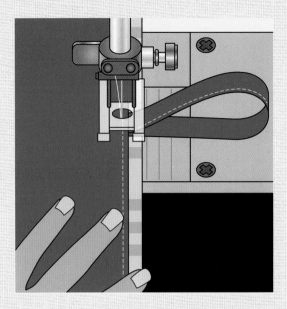

5. To turn the handle right side, pin a safety pin onto one end and then feed it through the handle and out the other end. Press the handle flat.

6. Take your small pieces for the loops and using a hot iron, press a 1 cm fold down each side to the centre, then fold over to the centre and press in half. Pin together and sew close to the folded edges. Repeat with the other loop.

7. Take your main bag piece and place it right side together (with the pocket on the inside). Pin along the two sides and sew 1 cm in from the edge using a straight stitch on your sewing machine. Repeat for the contrast coloured piece.

8. Around the top of the main fabric bag, press 2 cm to the wrong side, and around the top of the contrast bag, press 1 cm to the wrong side.

9. Turn the main fabric bag in the right way and leave the contrast bag inside out. Pin the handles at the side seams on the main fabric bag.

10. Find the centre of the top of the main fabric bag and pin the loops into place.

11. Place the contrast bag inside the main fabric bag, matching side seams. Pin around the top, noting that the contrast bag will peep 1/2 cm up from the top of the main fabric bag.

12. Sew the bags together around the top where you pinned, stitching close to the fold on the main fabric bag.

Now you can be a 'quick change artist' and amaze your friends with your interchangeable accessories!

Make-up bag

Every girl needs a handy bag to store her make-up, pens or current project supplies. No matter how many items you have, this bag can accommodate them all!

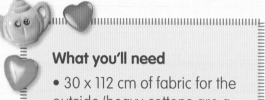

What you'll need

• 30 x 112 cm of fabric for the outside (heavy cottons are a good choice)

• 30 x 112 cm fabric for the lining

• 1 m cord for the tie

• Hand sewing needles

• Thread

• Sewing pins

• Fabric scissors

• Tape measure

1. From the outside fabric measure and cut:
One rectangle 25 x 35 cm (Piece #A)
One rectangle 25 x 23 cm (Piece #B)
From the lining fabric measure and cut:
One rectangle 25 x 35 cm (Piece #C)

2. Take piece #B on one of the 23 cm sides and fold a 1 cm edge under twice. Pin into place. Hand sew this hem using a running stitch.

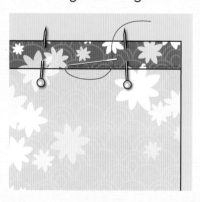

3. Place piece #A on a table with right side up, then layer on top piece #B (which you have just sewn) right side down, lining up the sides and the bottom edges. Layer on top piece #C (the lining), right side down. You now have a sandwich of three pieces, with the short piece in the middle.

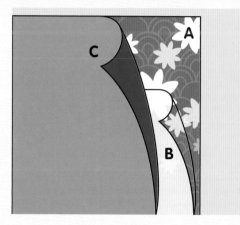

4. Pin through all layers along both long edges and the bottom edge, leaving the top edge open. Sew a straight line around where you have pinned, using a 1 cm seam allowance.

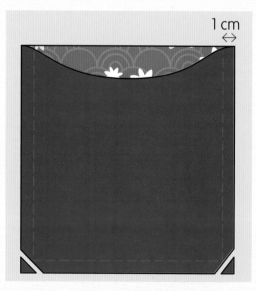

1 cm

5. Trim the bottom two corners and turn right side out.

6. Take the open edge and turn the raw seams in 1 cm. Use your fingers to press the edge and then pin the folds together. Hand stitch the two folded edges together using a running stitch.

7. Take your cord and tie a knot in the middle. Pin this knot to the edge of top centre back of your bag. Using double thread for strength, hand sew the knotted cord to your bag – make sure it is nice and strong!

Pack your things and roll up your bag. Well done! Your bag is complete!

Phone pouch

This pouch is simple and large enough to fit most mobile phones or iPods. Use materials you have around the house – even old jeans will work!

What you'll need

- 10 x 32 cm of fabric for the outside
- 10 x 32 cm of cotton fabric for the lining
- 10 x 32 cm of lightweight wadding (or an old face washer)
- 2.5 cm square of stick-on Velcro
- Sewing needles or a sewing machine
- Sewing pins
- 2B pencil
- Fabric scissors
- Contrasting embroidery thread

1. Place your phone on your fabric. The fabric needs to be 2.5 times the length of your phone, with 2 cm extra all round for seams. Measure, mark, and cut your lining, main fabric and wadding to the required measurements.

2. Place your main fabric and lining fabric right sides together. Layer the wadding on top of the wrong side of the main fabric. Pin the fabrics along three sides, leaving one short end open for turning.

3. Hand sew using a backstitch (or machine sew with a straight stitch), 1 cm in from the edge along the three edges where you have pinned. Remember to leave one short side open.

4. Trim away the wadding close to your stitching by sliding the scissors between the main fabric and the wadding. Don't trim the lining or outer fabric.

5. Carefully turn your pouch so that the right sides of the main fabric and the lining are showing and the wadding is now hidden inside.

6. Close up the open end by turning 1 cm of the lining, main fabric and wadding to the wrong side and pin.

7. Take the bottom edge of the pouch and fold it up 10 cm with the lining sides on the inside. Pin into place.

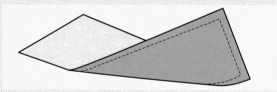

8. Sew around the outside using a contrasting embroidery thread.
Make sure to sew through all layers, all the way around. Give a couple of extra stitches where the 10 cm turn up finishes so that your pouch will be extra strong.

9. Pop in your iPod or iPhone to check where to place the Velcro. Peel and stick the Velcro into place. And your pouch is done! Why not text your friends and tell them what you have made?

Pocket organiser

Here's a handy way to get organised and recycle old items. Whip up this pocket organiser to give all your bits a home!

What you'll need

• Strong linen or a tea towel

• Pockets cut from old jeans or denim skirts

• Coloured thread – topstitch thread or embroidery cotton

• Pins

• Fabric scissors

• Piece of dowel or old curtain rod 20 cm longer than the width of your tea towel, or cord or string to hang

1. Cut the pockets from the jeans leaving a 1 cm border around the outermost stitching.

2. Shuffle the pockets on the tea towel until you are happy with how they look. Pin them into place. Keep the pins inside the pocket as you will sew the 1 cm border.

3. Use a feather stitch [page 18] and contrasting embroidery thread to sew your pockets onto the tea towel. Sew on the 1 cm gap around the pockets.

4. Make a casing at the top of your tea towel to thread your dowel or string. Turn the top edge over 4 cm or 5 cm (depending on the width of the dowel) and pin. Sew into place using a running stitch.

5. Put the rod through the casing at the top, tie the cord to each end and hang in a handy spot for you to use.

Optional:
Want to personalise your organiser? Just draw your design or words onto the tea towel and use any stitches you like to complete.

Tip
This organizer uses 6 pockets, but you can use more or less, depending on how many things you want to store!

Patchwork cushion

Mixing and matching prints and patterns is fun – this patchwork cushion cover will brighten up any room!

What you'll need

- 4 different fabrics with coordinating prints 12 x 45 cm
- Fabric for the cushion back 42 x 53 cm
- 40 cm cushion insert
- Three press studs (medium size)
- Matching thread
- Sewing machine
- Needles
- Sewing pins
- Fabric scissors
- Ruler or tape measure
- 2B pencil

1. For the patchwork pieces: With one selvedge closest to you and the fabric right side up, measure out a strip of fabric 12 x 45 cm. Mark measurement with a pencil and cut. Repeat with each of your different fabrics.

2. Pin your strips together, right sides facing, and use a 1 cm seam allowance and your sewing machine set on straight stitch to sew them together. If sewing by hand, use small running stitch.

3. Lay out your sewn pieces with the seams facing upwards. Press the seams to one side, then turn over and press your joined strips so that they lay flat.

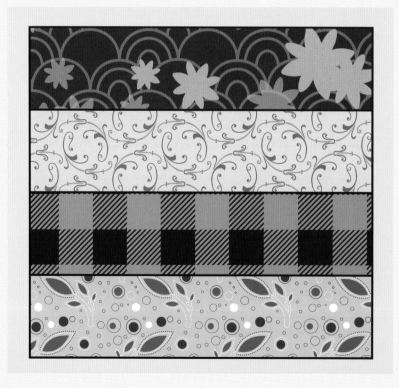

4. With the strips running horizontally in front of you, measure 12 cm wide lines, and mark with a pencil. Cut to make four strips, each with the four different fabrics in them.

5. Turn two strips upside down so that the patterns will contrast with each other. Pin the strips together, right sides facing, and making sure to line up the seams. Stitch together along one side, removing the pins as you come to them. If sewing by hand, use a small running stitch.

6. Pin the third strip to the two you have just sewn, and stitch. When you have stitched all four strips together you will have made a big square, Press the seams as in step 3.

7. Take one side of the square and edge it using a zigzag stitch on your machine, or a blanket stitch if hand sewing.

8. Press this finished edge under 1 cm then stitch a straight seam close to the zigzag edge. Use running stitch for hand sewing.

Hint
This method of patchwork is called 'strip piecing'

9. Take your backing fabric and zigzag or blanket stitch along one 42 cm edge. Turn the finished edge under 1 cm and stitch closed.

10. Take your patchwork square and your plain square and pin them together, right sides facing and matching all raw edges. The backing fabric will extend at one end to make the cushion 'flap'.

sides that you have just pinned. Give a little trim to remove any loose threads and turn right side out.

13. Finish off with three press-studs attached at the open end of the cushion to keep your cushion closed.

Insert a cushion, grab a book and make yourself comfy!

11. Turn your cushion cover over and pin the flap piece down, so that the fold of the flap is in line with the finished edge of your patchwork piece.

12. Using a 1 cm seam allowance, sew around the three raw edged

Personalised towel

Why not claim your favourite beach towel, and make your mark on it with a little creative sewing?

What you'll need

- Towel
- Fabric for appliqué (cotton or drill are good choices)
- Small piece of a medium weight iron-on interfacing
- Small piece of lightweight non iron-on interfacing
- Coordinating thread
- Paper scissors
- Sewing scissors
- Sewing pins
- Sewing machine
- Pencil and paper, or a computer to draw your design

1. Decide on the design you want to appliqué: Draw it or print it from your computer at the size you want to use.

2. Cut your paper design and pin it to the right side of your appliqué fabric. Keep the pins within the shape. Cut out the fabric design.

3. Lay out your iron-on interfacing with the shiny/sticky side facing up. With your fabric still pinned to the pattern, place it over the interfacing (the wrong side of the fabric down). Pin in place. Cut out your design from the interfacing.

4. Place your cutout appliqué on the ironing board. Place a press cloth or piece of cotton over the cutouts. Gently remove the pins and the paper pattern, without moving the pieces apart. Press together with a hot iron.

5. Pin your design into place on the towel.

6. Take a piece of non iron-on interfacing, large enough to fit around your pattern. Pin it to the back of the towel behind where your motif is placed.

7. Set your sewing machine to a wide zigzag, and your stitch length to just over the smallest setting. Experiment on a scrap of fabric to see what your zigzag looks like.

8. When you are happy with the look and pace of the zigzag, sew the appliqué design onto the towel. Go slowly – especially when sewing around corners. Make sure to remove the pins as you go!

9. When you have sewn around your design, cut away the interfacing from the back of the towel.

Now, take a long soak in the tub – you deserve it!

Chicken egg cozy

Boiled eggs are delicious – keep yours toasty warm with this quirky, cozy cover that you can make (almost) as quickly as you can boil an egg!

What you'll need

- Felt squares in colours of your choice (yellow, orange and red for this chicken)
- Sew-on or stick-on eyes, or buttons
- Matching sewing thread
- Hand sewing needle
- Sewing pins
- Fabric scissors and paper scissors
- Fabric glue (optional)

1. Use the template on page 78 to photocopy your pattern. Cut out two body shapes from your main colour, two wings from your second colour and a beak and a comb from your third colour.

2. Pin a wing on to each body and sew into place with two rows of running stitches, leaving the 'feathered' ends un-sewn.

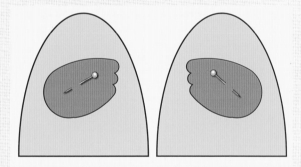

3. Sew or glue an eye onto each body piece.

4. Pin the two body pieces together and insert the comb and beak.

5. Sew into place by hand using a double running stitch all the way around your chicken. Make sure you leave the bottom end open.

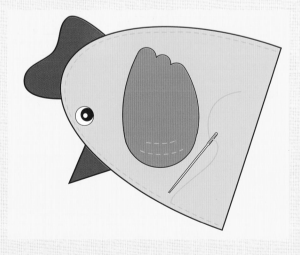

Eggs boiled? Toast cooked? Enjoy your breakfast!

Fragrant apples & oranges

Want to keep your room smelling great? All you need is a few pieces of cotton fabric, felt scraps and Potpourri!

What you'll need

- 30 x 30 cm square of red or orange fabric
- Small amount of cotton wool (or toy filling from a craft store)
- Potpourri
- Embroidery thread
- Ribbon
- Small pieces of felt for the leaves
- A large plate
- Sewing pins
- Fabric and paper scissors
- Needle and thread
- Pinking shears
- Pencil

1. Trace a large plate (approx 25 cm in diameter) onto your fabrics and cut out the circles using pinking shears. Use scissors to cut out the felt shapes for the leaves.

2. Hand sew a running stitch around the fabric shape 1 cm in from the pinked edge. Then gently pull the thread so that the fabric gathers a little. Do not cut off the thread.

3. Insert a small amount of toy stuffing to give the fruit some shape. Then fill up with Potpourri.

4. Pull the thread tight so that the fabric forms a round shape. Wind the thread around the top of the drawn-up fabric. Make some small stitches at different points around the top to secure it in place. Sew on the felt leaves and the ribbon.

Hang them in the wardrobe, or give them to a friend as a sweet-smelling gift!

Pretty amazing brooches

These quirky accessories are a great way to add colour to any outfit – make them in coordinated fabrics to jazz up the new clothes you have made!

What you'll need

- Felt squares
- Old beads, buttons and ribbons
- Sew-on eyes
- Small fabric scraps
- Colourful embroidery threads
- Scissors
- Sewing pins
- Cotton wool (or toy stuffing from a craft store)
- Brooch pins or safety pins
- A pencil (or chopstick)
- Hand sewing needles

Petal power

1. Use the templates on pages 79 and 80 to trace and cut out your patterns. Cut one large petal from felt and all other petals from fabric scraps. On a piece of contrasting felt, trace around a button and then cut out. Layer the fabric 'petals' over each other with the felt circle on the top.

2. Starting with a couple of firm backstitches on the back of your flower, push the needle through all layers to the front, and then from the front to the back.

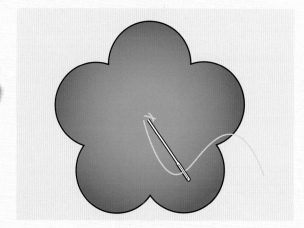

3. Lay your button on top of the felt circle. Sew through the buttonholes and through all layers of fabric to secure the button firmly in place.

4. Take your safety pin or brooch pin and place it at the back of your brooch. Sew through the brooch pin all the way through to the buttonholes at the front, then back again. Repeat a few times to make sure it is secure. Fasten off with three firm backstitches.

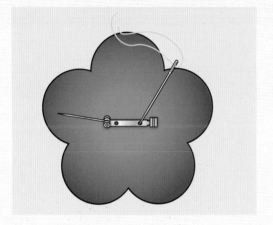

Lovely lady beetle

1. Use the template on page 80 to trace and cut out your pattern. You will need two wings cut from red felt, two bodies and six legs all cut from black felt.

2. Sew two small black buttons onto

each of the wings. Sew two eyes on to the top of the black felt oval (the upper body)

3. Attach the wings to the upper body using a running stitch. Sew legs to the under body using a backstitch.

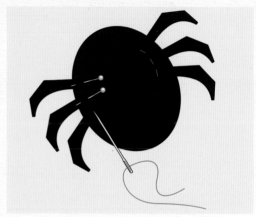

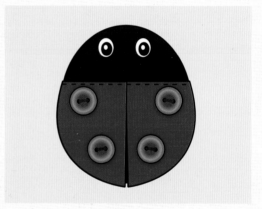

4. Stitch the upper body piece to the under body piece using a running stitch. Leave a 5 cm gap to insert the stuffing. Use a pencil or chopstick to push the filling in. Stitch the body parts together, making sure you leave the wings free.

5. Complete the stitching around the body, and sew on the safety pin or brooch pin.

Heart breaker

1. Use the template on page 80 to trace and cut out your pattern. Cut out two hearts from your felt.

2. Thread a large-eyed needle with a thin ribbon. Make sure you have enough beads or buttons to go around your heart shape. Thread the beads or buttons onto the ribbon, leaving 10 cm of extra ribbon at each end.

3. Thread another needle with thread. Stitch with a couple of backstitches at the upper centre back of one heart shape. Push the needle through the ribbon and, using a running stitch, sew the ribbon between each bead onto the felt. When you have sewn right around the heart, tie the ends of the ribbon to make a small bow.

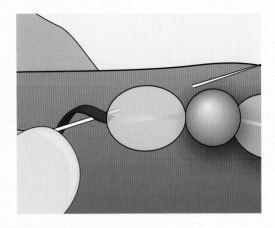

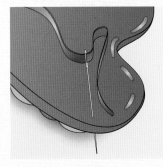

4. Thread a larger needle with a thicker piece of ribbon and, using running stitch, sew the two heart shapes together. Leave a small gap to insert the filling. Push the filling into the brooch, complete the stitching, and sew on a safety pin or brooch pin.

Superstar

1. Use the template on page 80 to cut out your pattern. Use this to cut out two stars from your felt.

2. Stitch beads or small buttons randomly and loosely onto one star.

3. Stitch the two stars together using a small blanket stitch. Leave a gap to insert the filling. Push the filling in and complete stitching around the star.

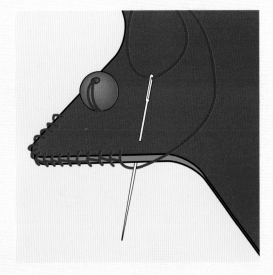

4. Sew on the brooch pin or safety pin and sparkle! You are a sewing star!

Pincushion

A pincushion is the safest place to keep your pins; this strawberry will keep your pins handy and available, as you can wear it around your wrist!

What you'll need

• Red and green felt (supplied with this book)

• Embroidery thread (supplied with this book)

• Small amount of polyester filling (or cotton wool)

• Stick-on Velcro spots

• Sewing needles with a large eye for embroidery

• Sewing pins

1. Photocopy or trace the templates on page 78 and 79 and cut them out. Then pin these onto your felt. Cut two strawberry bodies and one wrist band from red felt, and one leaf from green. Use a scrap of green to make the 'stalk'.

2. Split the embroidery thread into two groups of three strands each. Each length should be approximately 40 cm long. Thread your needle with one group of these three strands and make a knot at the end.

3. Pin the two pieces of felt strawberry bodies together. Begin sewing with three firm backstitches, then sew the seams together using a small running stitch along the two sides with the greatest curve.

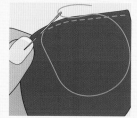

4. Thread your needle again with another three strands of thread, and make a knot at the end. Sew along each top of the strawberry body, being careful to sew through the join on each side. Sew right to the end, but don't cut off your thread, as you'll need this for the gathering.

5. Hold your strawberry in one hand, while you fill with the stuffing; make sure to push the stuffing right to the bottom.

6. When your strawberry is stuffed full, start to draw up the thread from around the top of the strawberry. Pull the thread tight and then use the remaining thread to sew the top of the strawberry together. Don't cut off the thread yet as you will need it to attach the leaf.

7. When the top of the strawberry is secure, push the needle up through the centre of your felt leaf and then down again to attach it to the top of your strawberry. Make a few

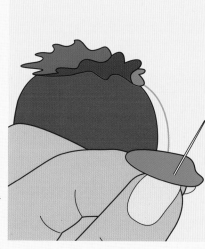

stitches to secure your leaf. Still with the same thread, take your piece of felt for the stalk and sew through one end to secure it to the centre of your leaf. Finish off with three firm backstitches underneath your leaf.

8. Fold the piece of felt that you cut for your wrist strap in half to find the centre. Pin the back of your strawberry to this centre mark.

Thread a needle with your remaining thread and make a knot in the end, and push your needle through the centre mark of the strap, through the strawberry and make a couple of backstitches. Stitch a line through the strawberry onto your strap, holding everything into place. Measure the wrist strap around your wrist and mark where the Velcro should go. Attach the stick-on Velcro where marked.

Congratulations – you can sew anything now!

Templates

CHICKEN EGG
COSY

CHICKEN EGG
COSY

CHICKEN EGG
COSY

CHICKEN
EGG
COSY

STRAWBERRY PINCUSHION

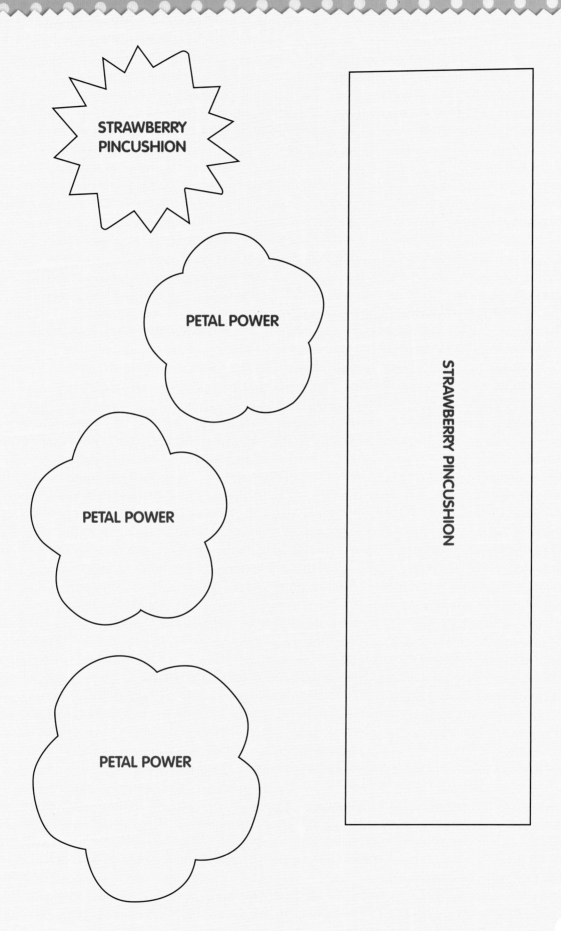

STRAWBERRY PINCUSHION

PETAL POWER

PETAL POWER

PETAL POWER

STRAWBERRY PINCUSHION

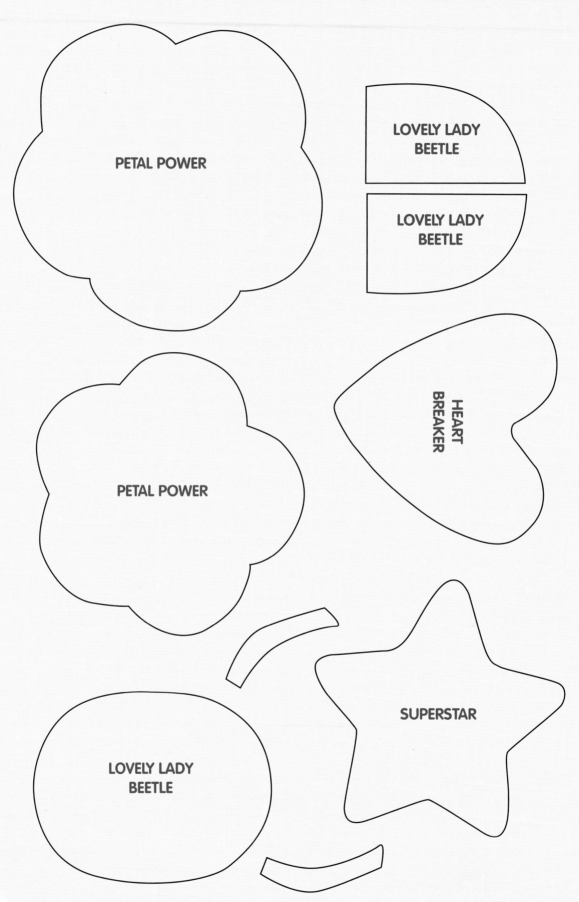

PETAL POWER

LOVELY LADY BEETLE

LOVELY LADY BEETLE

PETAL POWER

HEART BREAKER

SUPERSTAR

LOVELY LADY BEETLE